LOVE, LIFE & WILD LILIES

For You to Fall in Love with You - All Over Again!

Affirmation Diary From a Poet's Heart
-By Debjani Chaudhury

BLUEROSE PUBLISHERS
India | U.K.

Copyright © Debjani Chaudhury 2023

All rights reserved by author. No part of this publication may be reproduced, stored in a retrieval system or transmitted in any form or by any means, electronic, mechanical, photocopying, recording or otherwise, without the prior permission of the author. Although every precaution has been taken to verify the accuracy of the information contained herein, the publisher assume no responsibility for any errors or omissions. No liability is assumed for damages that may result from the use of information contained within.

BlueRose Publishers takes no responsibility for any damages, losses, or liabilities that may arise from the use or misuse of the information, products, or services provided in this publication.

For permissions requests or inquiries regarding this publication, please contact:

BLUEROSE PUBLISHERS
www.BlueRoseONE.com
info@bluerosepublishers.com
+91 8882 898 898
+4407342408967

ISBN: 978-93-5819-556-9

Cover design: Debjani Chaudhury
Typesetting: Debjani Chaudhury

First Edition: November 2023

Whispers of Hope

**A Poet's Journey Through Self-Love and Discovery
Hoping to Touch Your Soul, Too!**

Welcome to this journey of loving yourself, painted with vibrant hues of self-discovery, resilience, and the profound essence of self-affirmation.

The pages of this book yell about the transformative power of embracing one's flaws, the undulating journey from self-doubt to self-worth, and the unwavering resilience that blooms in the heart of the warrior in YOU.

This book is a part of my soul, adorned with verses that echo the journey of my evolution. It is a narrative woven from the threads of my own experiences—days drenched in uncertainty, where I was clawed by the demon of self-doubt, to the radiant dawn of empowerment and self-love that I am proud of today!

The ink upon these pages flows not just from a pen but from a wellspring of emotions—the days of tears to the ONE day when I decide to re-write my own destiny. Through the power of wordplay, I've etched my highs and lows, celebrating the mistakes that have embellished my journey, for it is these very missteps that lent the raw beauty of authenticity to my story.

This is the tale of my metamorphosis, and I hope to share the tiny ray of hope that fueled my journey to lighten up yours a little. I wish from all my heart that the words written somehow touch your soul or give you the self-acceptance you need in life. I dearly wish that this book helps you find that ONE day of your life when you get onto the steering wheel & ride past all judgments and self-doubt!

For within the folds of vulnerability lies the strength to explore, conquer, and reign in the beautiful world that awaits—a world waiting to be explored, embraced, and cherished.

I wish that my journey somehow resonates with your soul, igniting a spark that gives you the strength to accept each bit of your existence and flaunt it out loud — as that's where your journey will actually start!

With lots of love and light,
The Author,
Love, Life & Wild Lilies!

DECODING THE ESSENCE

"Love, Life, and Wild Lilies"

The intricate journey of self-discovery, resilience, and beauty within contrasts!

LOVE

Love, often associated with the affection we extend to others, here signifies a deeper narrative—the essence of self-love. It represents the journey of embracing oneself fearlessly, nurturing the roots of inner strength, and blossoming into a radiant being. It is the celebration of recognizing one's worth, acknowledging that self-love is the foundation upon which all other forms of love flourish.

LIFE

Life, within this context, signifies the canvas upon which our experiences are painted. It symbolizes the continual process of redefining our existence, embracing the highs and lows, and finding beauty in the unpredictability of our paths. Life, much like the wild lilies, thrives in contrast—a journey through the darkness that accentuates the brilliance of our resilience and growth.

WILD LILIES

The metaphor of Wild Lilies beautifully encapsulates the concept of thriving amidst adversity. Lilies, delicate and captivating, often flourish in the wild amongst the harshest conditions, yet their beauty shines brightly against the backdrop of adversity. Similarly, individuals like Wild Lilies find their strength and shine amidst life's toughest and most challenging circumstances. The contrast between their delicate appearance and their resilience mirrors the contrasting aspects of life itself—wherein, on the toughest paths, one discovers one's true essence and emerges stronger.

So, accept and acknowledge the wild, untamed aspects of your journey. Embrace your uniqueness, irrespective of the challenges, and find the courage to bloom fearlessly, standing out amidst the chaos!

Index

#1: Reaffirmation of Self-Love	10
#2: It's Okay to Pause and Unwind.	12
#3: Flaws are Beautiful.	14
#4: Free Your Spirit as the Wild Dandelions	16
#5: Embrace Your Journey	18
#6: Play Your Role Well	20
#7: Distinctiveness is Uniquely Liberating!	22
#8: Outgrow Your Shine with Pain	26
#9: Accept the Lying Truth	28
#10: Cease Chaos!	30
#11: Let Go..	34
#12: Manifest Self-Love	38
#13: Realize & Release	42
#14: Find Grey Amidst Mind vs. Love	46
#15: Trust the Process	50
#16: Keep Your Fight Mode On	54
#17: Numb Out Judgements	56
#18: The Strength of Attachment	58
#19: Broken is Always Beautiful	62

#20: Mask Off, Geisha!	66
#21: Circle of Life	68
#22: Hope Rooted with Reality	70
#23: Be Grateful	72
#24: Unleash the Inner Child	76
#25: Rise & Roar	80
#26: You Are the Lilium	82
#27: Spark the Revolt Within.	86
#28: Break Free!	90
#29: A Special Edition to Strengthen Parent-Child Relationship & Need to Communicate	94
#30: The True Essence	104

#1

Reaffirmation of Self-Love

You're a pretty force of nature.
Nothing ain't stopping you now!

Yes, before you start off on this journey of re-discovering yourself, let's reaffirm the strength within.

You have been through a lot, and time has always been your partner in healing it all for you. So, don't lose hope, and don't give up on yourself. You are beautiful. You are powerful. You are perfect. And nothing can stop you from rising again!

#2

It's Okay to Pause and Unwind.

The best plan at times is to have no plans at all,
To flow free-spiritedly with the stream,
not restricted by the wall.

Over-calculations can never save from the future's toll,
So just focus on giving the best shot and playing a fair role.

Anticipations are erroneous, as they can slip over the need of the present,
Remember, sudden clouds cannot take away the moon's luminosity, even if it is crescent!

It's okay to be an overthinker. It is okay to worry too much about your own. But, beautiful, is it important to bear the weight of the world on your delicate shoulders all through the day?

Take small breaks. You need it. Breathe in positivity. And breathe out the fear of the unknown. Trust the ultimate source.
Trust yourself. Trust your karmas. Remember, it will all be okay in the end. This, too, shall pass. Just wait for it and look out for yourself!

#3

Flaws are Beautiful.

The demons inside are also mine.
Accept the darkness within with a sip of wine.

And fight it right at the edge of the cliff.
Cause it's only the courageous you who can break
through the stiff.

Yes, the nascent you might feel that the world is
too bitter to survive;
But believe in yourself, raise your wings and create
the journey that you strive.

You, darling, have the fire within,
so never let the weakness in you sly.
Look inside to burn down the catapults to ashes as nothing,
but you decide how far to fly!

Empower your flaws, wear the scars as your badge of honor, and show your true self to the world - because you and only you decide your journey. Be proud of your imperfections as they define your beautiful identity. Ignite your inner will, gather your strength, channelize your energy cause you, my beauty, have just started. No one, absolutely no one, can burden you with their judgments.

Roar out louder as you,
and only you can decide how far you fly!

#4

Free Your Spirit as the Wild Dandelions

Time will free you from the mirage of negativity and diffidence.
All you need is to heal yourself with some love to hail with confidence!

The delicate dandelions across the sun-kissed fields will shine too.
Encompassing the compassion of the stars, sun, and the mighty moon!

Just believe that the wind will bear your success through the whispers of the sea.
Re-claim yourself, sealed with a promise not to let the grandeur of the crowd gloss over the simplistic beauty of being free!

Do you know the significance of a dandelion?

This small little flower encompasses the sun, moon, and stars too. The yellow flower represents the sun, the white puff ball represents the moon, and the dispersing seeds represent the stars. So, imagine the true power of this tiny blossom that literally encompasses the beauty of the entire universe within itself. So, never underestimate.

You, darling, are just like this beautiful bloom.
Your energies are unbelievably strong. You hold the universe within too. Just channel your will, believe in yourself, and go rule the world with confidence!

#5

Embrace Your Journey

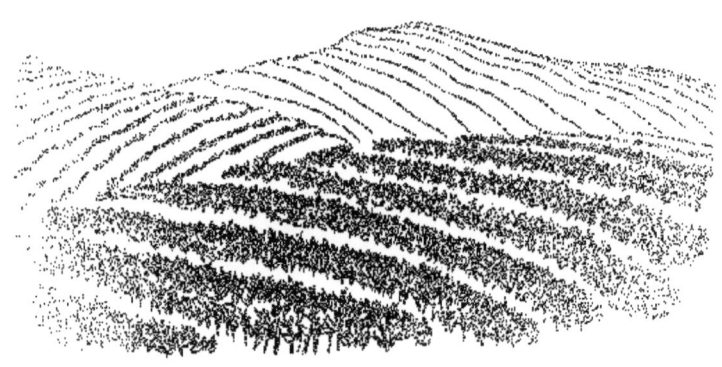

Your journey is nothing beyond the
compilation of your deeds,
Of memories, decisions, and the future's seeds!

The amalgamation of situations,
the rights and wrongs will heed;
The life of greys, smiles, and teary eyes that bleed.

Your journey could be as bitter as
the sweet sugar plum indeed;
All you need is to own yourself and the journey you lead.

It's for no one but you to accept the golden
harvest happily or for two rots reseed;
But, remember darling, black or white, your journey
is yours very own to grow, repent, or feed!

Life has its share of fun to have - to test you with bitter and sweet experiences. Let it enjoy too. Crib less. It's okay!

Remember, no one, absolutely no one, walking on the pathway outside your home is free of sadness and problems. It's all about how you bat those problem-balls thrown at you by life and circumstances. So, just be on your toes, give it all your passion, and leave the rest for destiny to decide. Just feel and enjoy every bit of your journey - pain, happiness, experiences and loss. However they are, they are all a part of you. So own up for all of them
- proudly and strongly!

#6

Play Your Role Well

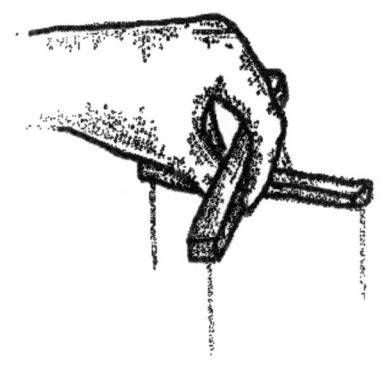

We are nothing but puppets in the hands of time,
Seeing the dark empty hall or smiling through
the audience's clappy chime.

Death is the ultimate, inevitable reality of life,
Age remains the real marionette that can be
cut with no knife.

It's always like time slipping through your fingers
as the rough sand,
All you have to do is put up the show with an empty smile,
so grand.

Each day is a new matinee to rejoice with your own,
As tomorrow you could be alone holding up
the stage in the terrain unknown!

Let's face it - nobody knows tomorrow.

Nobody can predict it, and nobody can control or manipulate results. We are true puppets in the hands of time and this universe. So, all that's in your tiny hands and will is to give life your best shot!

Live each moment. Re-assure yourself of today's satisfaction and 'flow with the flow.' Nothing is permanent; nothing is your own except YOU. So, enjoy your part, love yourself, and play it well. Have fun. Leave no regrets for tomorrow. Rest, everything that went wrong, time will take care of it.

Space out and heal!

#7

Distinctiveness is Uniquely Liberating!

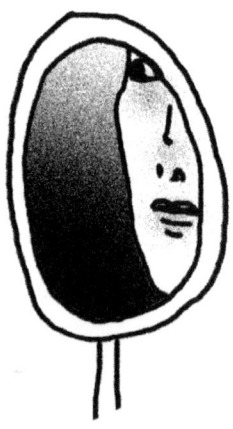

Ostriches are not expected to fly altitudes to cross dunes.
Cranes are not meant to be grounded but fly high
over the cloudy fumes!

All of us are uniquely built with beautiful weaknesses
and unmatchable boons.
Just need the magical wand to believe in yourself
and fly out of the restrictive cocoon!

You are the mirror of your self-esteem, so unleash yourself
and rule the world like the last-ever queen of this Rangoon!

Chase uniqueness and not crowd.

Turn your silence into your strength as you weave your story through inner willpower. Each one is uniquely able to rule the world with hidden talents and strengths. So, don't get stuck in the endless loop of comparisons and negativities. Carve your own destiny, and write your own story. Don't let anyone define who you are.

Be un-tamed.
Be un-typical. Be-you!

#8

Outgrow Your Shine with Pain

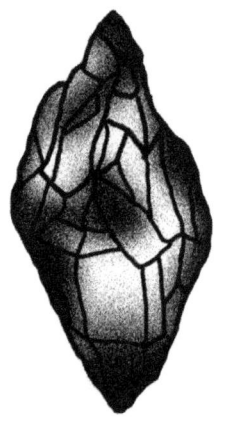

It's okay to have too many harsh phases in life;
Remember that your shine is determined by
how hard you've strife.

Brilliant cut diamonds have the maximum broken edges,
shining brightest of all;
As they have a multitude of luminous facets that
light up the darkest hall.

So, if times are hard, you are on your way to
being polished for the ultimate glory;
The stronger you fight, the brilliance in your eyes
will tell a greater story!

Remember, exceptional is never easy.

Extraordinary always has a story to tell. And stories are never complete without pain or challenges. So, cheer yourself up as you walk your rainy path, as these thunders of pain are yelling for an extraordinary climax to come!

You are the diamond. You are a legacy of strength. Identify your dreams and chase them harder, as your story is all set to prevail. Get yourself together and push harder once again. And, quit the very thought of quitting.
The best is yet to come, darling!

#9

Accept the Lying Truth

Our well of truth might be as shallow as deep;
Filled with fear of judgments swallowing down each weep.

Truth is a delusional sense of perspective struck hard within.
Overshadowed by fear of loss or deep-rooted
love pulling down the chin!

Sometimes, we drown in the unknown to escape acceptance.
But the face of truth will haunt back every time
to seek the due reflectance!

So own your truth to the last bit of your life,
Because lying about your existence is the worst strife!

Yes, situations drive our life, but trying to be desirable is the worst punishment you can give yourself. It's like insulting your soul with a lie that will cost you your self-respect. People might have multiple perceptions about you, don't let that bother your confidence, will or dreams.

It's just about how you start admiring yourself and accepting your truth.
You are perfect the way you are.
Full Stop.

#10

Cease Chaos!

The hustle-bustle of today's chaotic world is a myth;
A dark den that sees no ray of light at the end of the filth.

Yes, the muck in our hearts has blinded us to win this rat race of success;
Forgetting the fact that we are mouse-trapped in the pressure full circle of regress.

This race to excel has no finish line to find
the happy ending of this chase;
So why noose yourself in this covet to become the best face?

The focus should be to become the best version
of yourself instead;
A simple pause to reflect on the beauty of nature
can free you from all your dread!

In a world that often glorifies chaos and relentless ambition, it's extremely important to recognize that the pursuit of external success can trap us in a never-ending race.

Instead, darling, choose to focus on nurturing your inner self and evolving into the best version of who you are.

It is important to find solace in the simplicity of self-reflection and reconnecting with the beauty of nature, which frees each soul from the pressures and anxieties of the rat race. Choose the path of self-discovery and contentment rather than choking yourself up in the pursuit of external validation. You are complete the way you are. Just keep refining your actions towards the vision of freeing out the best version of yourself!

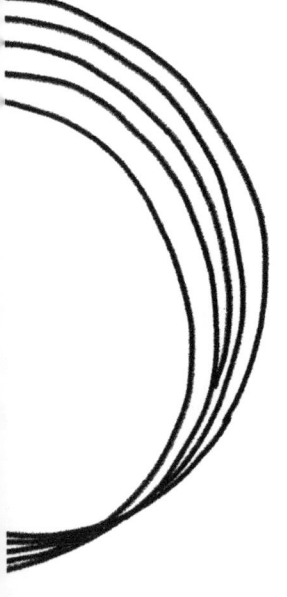

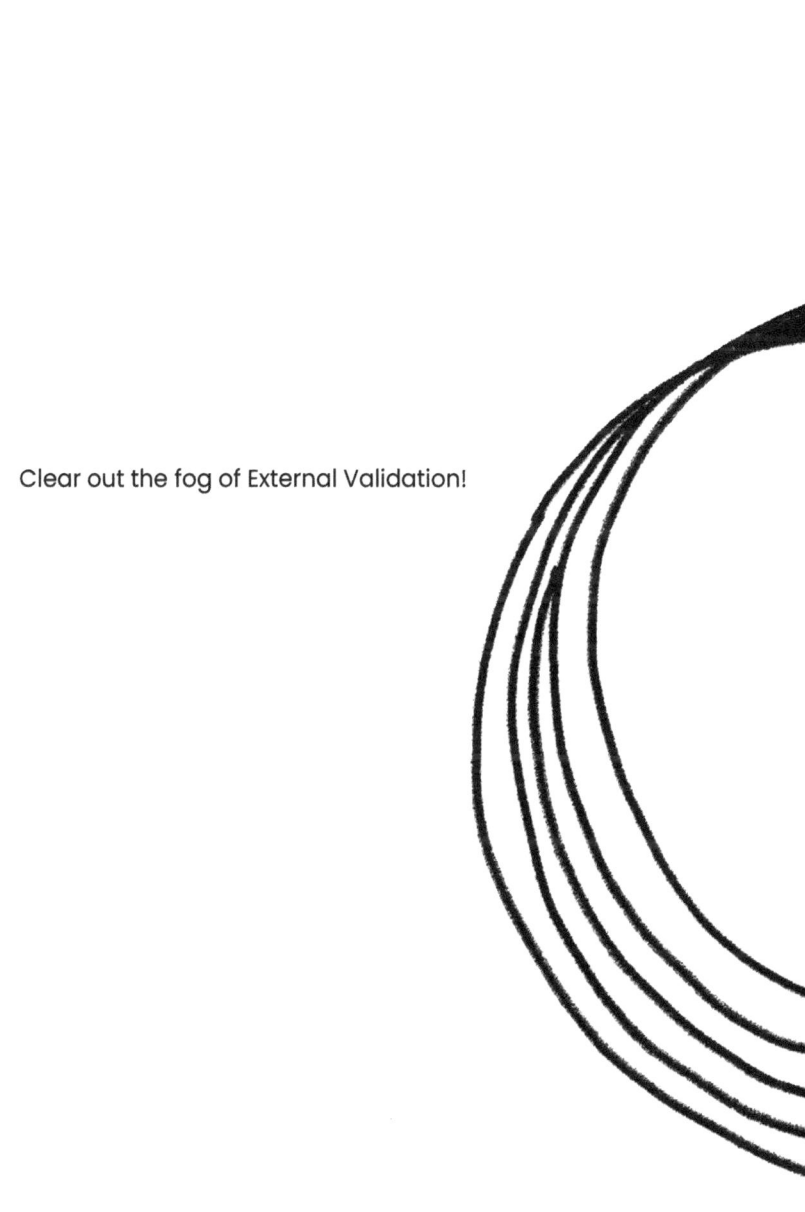

Clear out the fog of External Validation!

#11

Let Go..

Colorful exuberance that lights up the dull, lifeless skies;
Filling up our lives with the adrenaline rush as high as it flies.

The joy of togetherness tied up in the little
too delicate thread called 'love'.
A kite is not too different from the life full Dove.

It teaches us too many life-enriching lessons, though.
Showing us how too hard a grip can make
the flight of this beauty your foe.

The brightest things in life usually demand
space to shine on their own.
It's best to let them decide their path up in the
distant sky or way back home!

The risk of the bonded kite getting its roots slashed on the way will always stay.
But trust your will; if your bond is strong enough, it will make storms sway in an unexpected way!

Your relationships with loved ones are akin to the colorful kite in the sky, teaching you the invaluable lesson of letting go and trusting destiny. Just as a kite can never be controlled, understand that you must release the fear of loss and trust that what is meant for you will return in its own time.

Remember, do not suffocate yourself or lose your identity in the pursuit of gaining or keeping someone else in your life.

Like the kite, the brightest aspects of life require space to shine, and you need to allow your relationships the freedom to find their own path. Though there may be risks and storms on this journey, have faith that a strong bond will navigate them in unexpected and beautiful ways. Don't burden yourself. Don't let fear of loss ever rule. Ultimately, remember, the kites that return home are the only ones who are meant to be yours!

#12

Manifest Self-Love

Manifest your happiness as that's what you deserve ..
Remember that you are the sole source of your verve!

Don't let anyone's voice pull down your
self-confidence with dearth,
As no one but only you can decide your true worth!

Let the world's wordsmith pass by as purposeless déjà vu,
Cause nothing can define you better than you!

In the journey of life, accept that your self-worth and confidence are solely defined by your perception of yourself. Never let external voices diminish your inner strength or create self-doubts.

**Maybe you are just
feeling lost as you let someone overshadow
your understanding of yourself.**

Stop. Pause. Re-align!

Remember, you are the author of your story, immune to the superficial judgments of the world. No one, absolutely no one, is better suited to define your true essence and worth than yourself. Let your self-love guide you. Manifest your true potential and happiness in every step of this beautiful journey. And that's where you will find your true self!

#13

Realize & Release

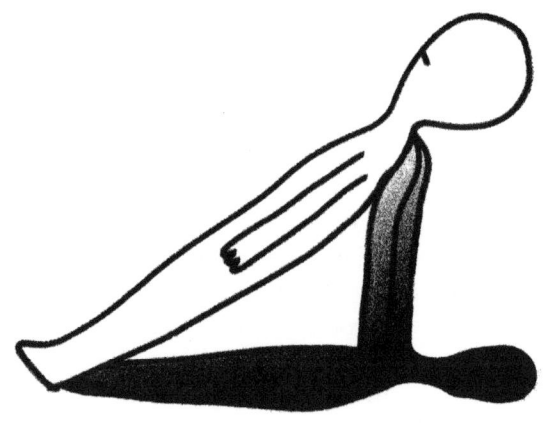

Don't let your mistakes shadow your actions to make you who you are!

Get ready! It is time to recognize your past experiences, both the ones that you are aware of and the ones you may not fully understand. Don't dodge.

Acceptance is the key!

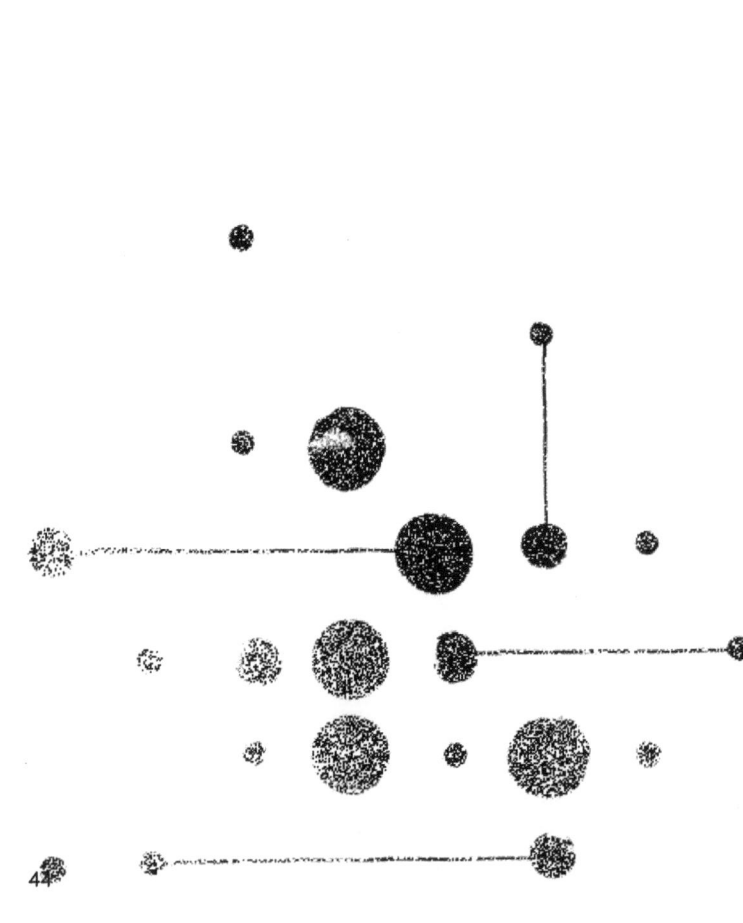

Remember, these experiences are the ones that have woven the fabric of your present and will influence your future just as the mistakes and challenges of your past have shaped you. They also remind you of the strength and resilience you carry within.

Darling! Understand that it's crucial to acknowledge, learn from, and, when necessary, release the burdens of your past in order to fully embrace the present and create a brighter, more fulfilling future. Through self-awareness and forgiveness, you can transform the shadows of your past into valuable lessons that will guide you toward a more empowered and purposeful life.

Acceptance will help you open the doors to happiness. **So, set yourself free of your past!**

#14

Find Grey Amidst Mind vs. Love

Mind is man's greatest enemy to befriend,
Overcalculations that distort reality for the unpredictable end.

The games of the mind over love are worse than the ones for the throne,
Making the heart break through the loop of questions for the urge of the unknown!

Mind lacks sheer gratefulness about today,
Busy calculating the returns for tomorrow's gay.

Life is no black or white, so choose the Grey blissful imperfection,
As the perfect way is to mark gratitude and not miss out on your heart's conviction!

Yes, you are a beautiful soul with
a lot of love to share.

So, share fearlessly!

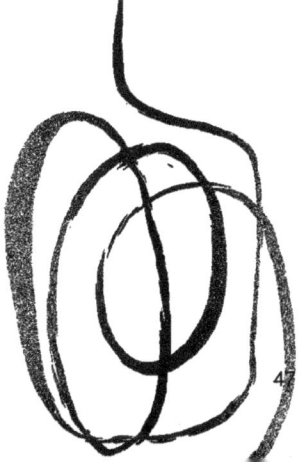

Remember, in matters of love,
the tendency to let emotions rule and seek to
predict the future will always stay.
But acknowledge that calculations and
overthinking will surely distort your
current happiness.

Recognize that the mind's overanalysis can often
become your worst enemy, leading to
unnecessary questions and uncertainties.
So, open your heart. Embrace the wisdom in
finding the grey area where imperfections and
gratitude coexist in blissful harmony. Love is not a
game of calculations but a journey of the heart.
Therefore, choose to appreciate the present and
trust your heart's convictions.

**So, let go of the need for a perfect end and
embrace the beauty of life's unpredictable path.
Enjoy the present and travel through the future with
lots of love and acceptance!**

#15

Trust the Process

Trust is just like the floating bubbles on the sea waves,
That can burst out with overlapping slaps of truth, but be brave.

Hold on to your self-belief even if they seem vague;
Cause none can crack through the other's mind to understand what is unsaid.

So let time show the reality of your relationship and what memories made;
Love seeks no replacements by the worth of your partner weighed.

The fragility of relationships is its true beauty that could trade;
But finding solace somewhere unknown can slaughter your bond like a sharpened blade!

Love is nourishing. Love teaches you the true lessons of self-prioritization!

It is important to believe in this beautiful process of attachment, understanding that time has its own way of reflecting the truth within relationships. Each individual is unique, and it's important to grant them the time and space to reveal themselves, allowing the unsaid to unfold naturally. Love isn't about seeking alternatives; it's about embracing the growth of a unique connection.

We all are bubbles in this ocean of love, bursting for some waves while flowing through the others.

Love liberates and sets our souls free to grow and shine from within.

So, protect your emotions and nurture the growth of love, trusting in the purity of this process. Just as bubbles on the sea waves may burst, you have to be brave and true to your self-belief, for the journey of love is a path of beauty and vulnerability that should be cherished rather than replaced or taken for granted. The bubbles that are meant to burst will diminish, but let them elevate your inner self till the time they exist. That's the process you need to trust. That's the process that will elevate your soul. We all are bubbles in this ocean of love, bursting for some waves while flowing through the others.

#16

Keep Your Fight Mode On

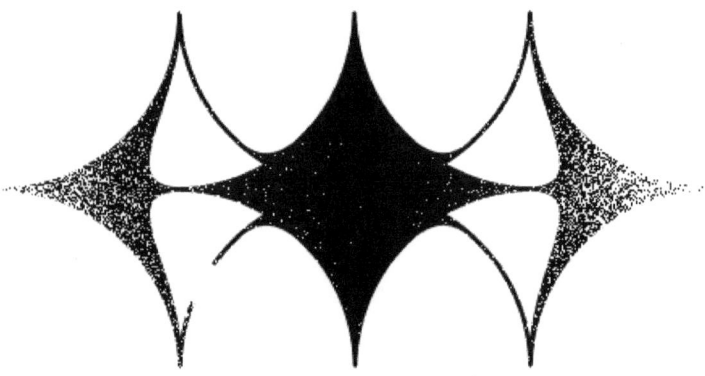

Stars are wired to direct us to play on the
tunes of destiny's call;
Aiming for the bling up in the sky helps you
cross all your barriers and walls!

But remember, your dreams are bigger than destiny's mission;
Cause you can change what's written with
your hard work and vision.

No matter how cloudy your journey gets with
situations turning unpredictably untamed;
What matters is that you need to continue hustling, wearing
your failures on your chest - unashamed!

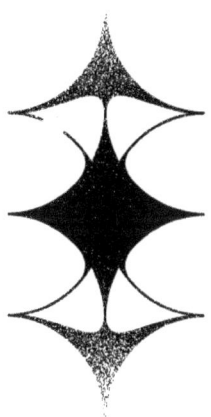

My little Herculean soul, in this war called life, it is time for you to affirm your unwavering commitment to keeping your fight mode ON. It is time to erase the tiniest possible streak of self-doubt.

With hard work and a clear vision, you will have to use the untamed power to rewrite the narrative of your life. Even when faced with cloudy and unpredictable situations, you will persist, wearing your failures as badges of honor, unashamed. The journey may be challenging, but you have to be determined to overcome all barriers and walls, aiming for the shining stars in the sky and embracing the call of destiny with resilience and unwavering strength. You are way bigger than the hurdles in your life. So, every time you fall, get up and remember to aim higher.

Never underestimate yourself by overestimating your target!

#17

Numb Out Judgements

Mirror, Mirror on the wall, who's the most beautiful of them all?
The eyes that schemingly scan your fats?
Or the voice telling you to be fair and tall?
Or is it the one who created the great
body image issues wall?
The answer to what defines a perfect body is drowned in the melancholy aimed at making you feel small!

What if the greatest princess questioned her self-worth and didn't go to the ball?
Sometimes disillusioned by the world's noise can make you lose what's written in destiny's call.
So wear your glass shoes on and walk with your chin up as you are the beauty that needs no thrall!

A promise you need to make to yourself today is that - you will numb out judgments that pull your morale down!

You need to recognize that the definition of beauty should not be dictated by critical eyes, demeaning voices, or societal pressures that create body image issues. Learn from our childhood fairytales to unleash the lovely fairy in you. Never question your self-worth and understand that disillusionment with the world's noise can obscure the path written in destiny's call.

Choose to embrace your unique beauty, regardless of external expectations or judgments, and walk with your chin held high, for you are the embodiment of beauty that requires no validation from others. Your self-worth is rooted in self-acceptance and the belief in your intrinsic value!

#18

The Strength of Attachment

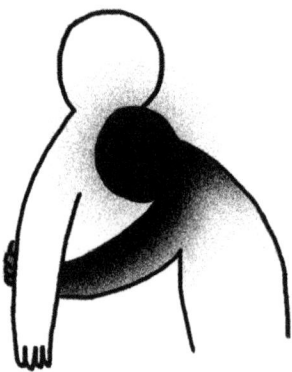

Attachment is a liability or an asset to reclaim;
Does it turn down as a weakness that you cannot blame?

Or give you the will to outshine yourself for your own?
To prove thy worth and make the person happy by transitioning life to his zone?

But once you shift in, do things still remain the same?
The fear of loss leaves nothing like yourself in you other than your name!

Attachment is not a synonym for being an add-on to someone's existence,
But to find support and zeal to be a better version of yourself with persistence.

Attachment should give you the power to build the dynasty of your dream.
And not let your hard-earned cottage wash down with your teary stream!

Repeat out & loud..

"I affirm that the strength of attachment should empower me, not weaken me. It's solely my choice to determine whether attachment becomes a liability or an asset in my life. And I will choose wisely. I will choose for myself!"

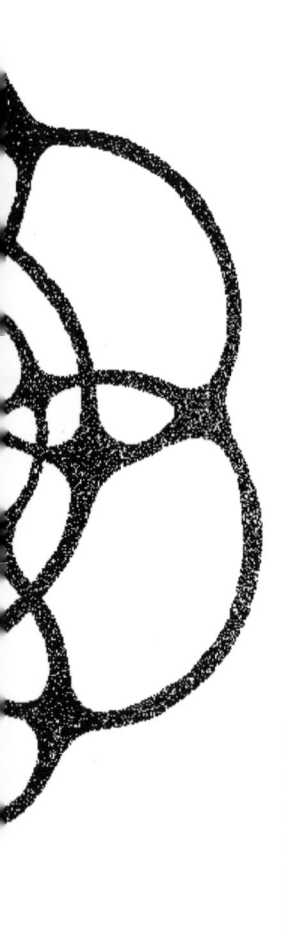

It is time for you to understand that it's not about becoming a mere add-on to someone's existence but about finding support and inspiration to enhance yourself and become a better version of who you are. Attachment should provide you with the courage to pursue your dreams and build a dynasty of your own. Don't let the tears you shed for others take a toll on your happiness. Choose to approach attachment with the mindset that it contributes to your growth and the fulfillment of your aspirations, making you even more resilient and determined.

So choose yourself above the rest always!

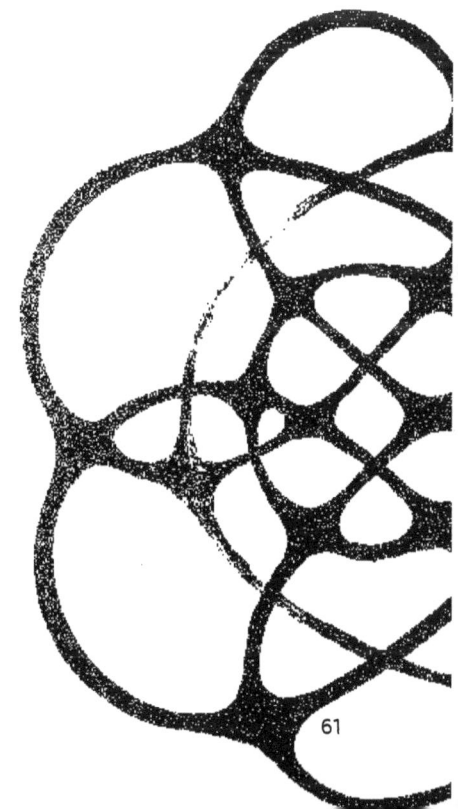

#19

Broken is Always Beautiful

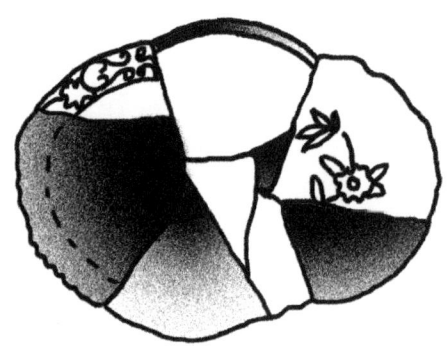

You might win the greatest war right when you
are on your knees surrendering,
People misjudging your strength can
re-establish your need for winning!

The art of kintsugi can make you a masterpiece with each of
your failed broken bits sealed with confidence;
All you need is the never-fail attitude to give yourself a second
chance to prove your provenance!

Every closed door on your face is a step closer to your
ultimate archway to success!
Remember that your lowest failure could set free your
fears for ultimate liberation from societal suppresses!

Always remember in moments of surrender and vulnerability, true strength emerges. Understand that the misjudgment of your abilities by others can serve as a catalyst for you to reaffirm your determination to succeed.

Just like the art of kintsugi, you can transform your broken pieces into a masterpiece, mending them with confidence and resilience. It's time for you to embrace the attitude that will allow you to give yourself a second chance, affirming your unique journey and origin. Each closed door on your path brings you one step closer to the ultimate gateway of success. So, recognize that your lowest failures are opportunities for personal growth and liberation from societal constraints. Your journey, with all its flaws and mends, is a testament to your inner strength and the beauty of self-belief and resilience.

So, get up, join your broken pieces of failures, fix your soul and get back stronger than ever!

#20

Mask Off, Geisha!

"The more the colors, the better your triumphant stage presence," they proclaim.

Hiding away your true identity and swallowing your existence behind the paint masking your essence is the game!

Why does fitting into the world's expectations make one shift colors and roles unknown?

Changing costumes, characters, and roles - do you recognize yourself in the mirror alone?

We are all geishas performing to the tunes of society to please,

Crying through the samisen seeking acceptance to set free our true character and not seize!

The world is too crowded to find acceptance for your distinguishing character, but be real.

Don't trespass your self-belief, as the race to win over claps from the audience is just surreal.

It's time to make a few promises to yourself!

Commit to embracing your true self without hiding behind masks or conforming to societal expectations. Understand that the world may encourage you to don various colors and roles, but refuse to lose sight of your identity in the process. We all are Geishas, as we've often played roles to please society. But you've to learn that true acceptance lies in being authentic. You need to no longer sacrifice your self-belief for temporary applause from the audience.

Instead, choose to break free from the performance at societal tunes and seek your own path, guided by the unwavering light of your true character, unmasked and unafraid to shine as who you truly are. So, put the masks off, my Geishas!

#21

Circle of Life

The mystic beauty of the circle defines human life,
Running behind advancing goals as nothing can ever suffice.

Wish satisfaction was not a myth to chase;
Wish happiness was linear and straight with some pre-defined base.

But happiness, like a circle, has no end;
Needs vs. Wants is what makes the circle of life at each point bend.

In this never-ending circumference of success, don't forget the epicenter of your existential cause.
All you need is to reflect on your journey, realign your ultimate goals, and take a pause!

Life's beauty lies in its cyclical nature, where we often chase ever-advancing goals, realizing that true satisfaction can be elusive. You must wish for linear happiness with a defined base, as it is important to embrace the idea that happiness, like a circle, has no end.

The dance between needs and wants continually shapes the circle of life at every point. Amid this never-ending journey, don't forget the core of your existence; don't forget your ultimate goal. You must reflect on your path, realign your actions, and take moments to pause and appreciate this cyclical journey that defines the essence of human life.
It is important to find contentment in the process rather than solely chasing the destination.

Remember, sometimes, journeys are more beautiful than destinations!

#22

Hope Rooted with Reality

A broken heart flies as light as a feather;
Driven directionlessly by the force of the weather.

Is it the feeling of liberation or the void of
desperation that leads?
Seeking to escape the present or rub off
with blame on deeds?

Vulnerability has a strength of its own to discover;
Only if you look inside yourself for support and not depend on
others to console and recover.

Cause the feather flies holding on to a delicate rope called 'hope',
where the blame game can take a toll.
Erase expectations from your ally and sing to the tunes of
self-love that perches deep in your soul!

In vulnerability lies the true strength!

When your heart feels broken and adrift, it's time to acknowledge that the vulnerability it brings carries its unique strength. Understand that escaping the present or placing blame on past actions will not lead to genuine liberation or healing. Instead, recognize the importance of seeking support within rather than depending on external sources for consolation and recovery.

Like a feather holding onto the delicate rope of hope, choose to let go of the blame game and focus on self-love. Understand that real hope is rooted in reality, where expectations are erased. So, find solace by nurturing your inner self, allowing it to take deep root within your soul, and encouraging self-growth.

Identify the beauty of hope and help it heal you!

#23

Be Grateful

Gratitude is what churns sufficiency from bare incompleteness;
Dissatisfaction, driven by the fear of the unknown and the stubbornness to excel, creates restlessness.

The yardstick of comparison with the rest is scattered away in the real world;
The competitiveness injected in our blood streams makes all our straight thoughts jumbled and curled!

Excellence is a virtue to rejoice if gratitude is not subtracted from the equation.
Be realistic and enjoy your gradual growth with gratitude rather than longing to be an overnight sensation!

Close your eyes, take a deep breath, and try to relive your journey. Remember all the hardships, remember all the challenges that led you to who you are today. Realize the significance of being grateful for every achievement and milestone along your journey.

Remember, gratitude is the catalyst that transforms what may seem incomplete into sufficiency. It's important to understand that dissatisfaction often stems from the fear of the unknown and the relentless pursuit of success, leading to restlessness.

Embrace the idea that comparison and competitiveness can blur the path to excellence, making it essential to untangle your thoughts and focus on the uniqueness of your journey.

Brace yourself. Brace your journey!

Take pride in your progress and celebrate each step, for excellence is truly a virtue that should be enriched with gratitude. Choose to be realistic and find joy in your gradual growth, appreciating your journey.

Overnight successes are a myth.
True glory lies in growth!

#24

Unleash the Inner Child

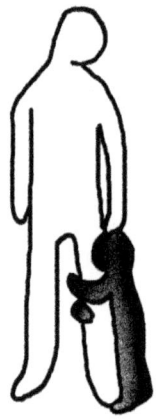

Running around the veranda across the sun-kissed lemon tree;
Hiding behind the old car parked, yet to discover the reality of the world, felt so free!

The falls back then had only physical harm, with wounds bleeding;
Unlike the hard world of grownups where you step onto others for exceeding!

Those good old days were called 'the true celebration of life.'
If growing up didn't feel like a bane, one could cease their childhood with a roll of fife!

As a child, we push really hard to get our views validated as grown-up adults.
Wish that we could go back to these golden memoirs to escape reality with the child-like occult!

It is important to unleash the inner child within you, setting it free from the complexities of the adult world. Pause for a while and recall the joy of running under the sun, the thrill of hiding and the fearless exploration of life's mysteries. In those moments, the wounds were only physical, unlike the harsh realities of adulthood. And cherish those days as the true celebration of life, where growing up didn't feel like a burden but rather a joyful journey. With the same zeal, accept your failures, stand up again and try harder!

Strike back to reality, where, as an adult, you are stuck in the mess of gaining societal validation. Break through it. Choose to unapologetically embrace your inner child, allowing it to reignite the sense of curiosity, innocence, and playfulness. Don't let the child in you suffocate with the burdens of the society. Set it free. Allow it to fall and get up every time. Cherish its vulnerabilities.

Let it breathe and grow!

#25

Rise & Roar

> Hey, I am Cavil the majestic wall,
> Yes, the one who stands great and tall
> Ruling the dumb minds of all
> Conspiring judgements and perceptions to make you fall
> Are you ready to hear my call?

> Knock, knock!

> Hell No, damsel in distress is too cliché
> I'd rather drive through your lofty objections
> in my pretty Porsche

> I am beyond the mindless versions, assertions, and perceptions
> Of limited knowledge, aggravated with
> aggression, expection and possession
> I have broken through the chains of
> perfection, aspiration, and supression
> On a journey to infinite creation, succession, and liberation

> My mind is elevated by my will to surpass
> the climate of opinion
> As I have built a wall-less empire of passion
> stepping over your mindless dominion

It is time for you to rise and roar against Cavil, the mindset block and break the wall of judgements that often make you feel incomplete or small. You need to understand the importance of not letting such judgements inject self-doubt into you.

Stand up and choose to confront and challenge Cavil with confidence, driving through his objections in your metaphorical Porsche of self-assurance.

You've transcended the limitations set by society. Break free from the chains of perfection, aspiration, and suppression. Your journey is marked by the pursuit of liberating your true self. You have to elevate your mind by refusing to be confined by the climate of others' opinions, building a wall-less empire of passion that stands as a testament to your resilience, determination, and unwavering self-belief!

#26

You Are the Lilium

Here goes the saga of a flower, so colorful
Vividly lighting up lives with a smile so powerful

'Lillum' was her name as she soared up high through the thick, thorny wilds
Her bounty packed by tendrils dreamt of touching the skies

Little did she know where her destiny would take
As beautifully tied to her enigma in a bouquet she walked by a lake

A hope that the journey was taking her to a romantic stage
Little did she know would lie up as a reminiscence to someone's grave

Yes, she did sob a little as her wishes had a part to play in making someone merrier
But, for destiny's song she marked eternity over the role of some temporary spear carrier

Yes, the beautiful Lilium couldn't mark her presence in porcelain so exquisite
But, she did spell a lifetime of Mr. Crimson keeping him alive in hearts to reinspirit

In the captivating story of life, we are all Lilium,
with our own ambitions & wants. Lilium, much like each of us,
traversed through thorny paths, her tendrils reaching for the
skies, harboring dreams beyond the confines
of her existence.

Her journey took an unexpected turn as she yearned to grace
a romantic proposal bouquet, only to find herself nestled
beside Mr. Crimson's final resting place. Initially, this twist
evoked a sense of sadness, a fleeting sorrow, very similar to
the disappointments we encounter when life
doesn't work our way!

Lilium's tale mirrors the aspirations and dashed hopes that often befall our ambitious souls. Despite the initial dismay, Lilium's presence next to Mr. Crimson's grave became a symbol of eternal remembrance. Though she couldn't adorn exquisite porcelain or be a part of a joyous celebration, her role transcended that of a temporary adornment.

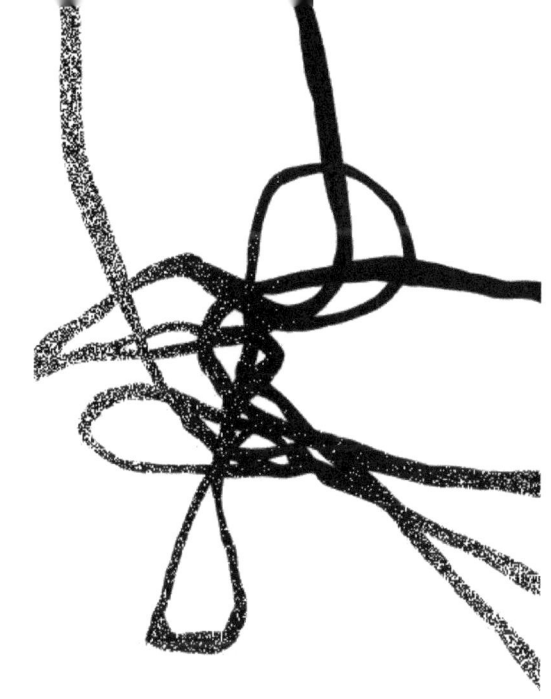

Embrace the essence of Lilium within you.
Amidst life's unpredictability and unmet expectations, remind yourself that setbacks and detours may lead to unforeseen and greater destinations. Trust in the orchestration of destiny, for it weaves tales that surpass fleeting desires, unveiling a deeper purpose that awaits your discovery.

You are the Lilium—an unbreakable force amidst life's twists and turns. Embrace the unknown with unwavering faith, for within it lies the potential for a destiny far grander and more impactful than your initial aspirations. Trust in the unseen hand guiding your journey, for it holds the promise of a narrative that transcends your wildest dreams!

#27

Spark the Revolt Within.

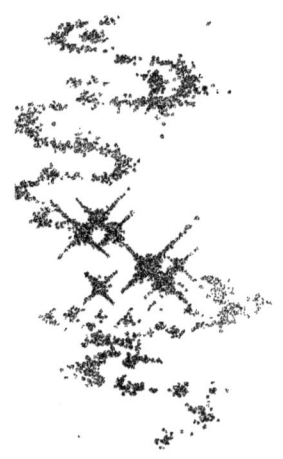

Revolution is not magnificence
It's just a courageous spark caught off defense.

A tiny will to empower the timid,
A mountainous zeal to do the untrodden, leaving all livid.

Yes, the revolution starts with a little thought
that pops your heart,
A disagreement to adjust to things that are known to fall apart.

It's all about standing strong to the version you want to portray,
Ditching what seems serene white for the world,
to choose your grey!

And, fight for it till the very last gasp of breath
 for your hot blood to flow
A rush of no regrets as you give it all till the very last blow!

Believe in what you know is right, even if it's just a small feeling deep within. It's that courage to stand up for what you believe, empowering not just yourself but those around you who hesitate. Revolution isn't about big gestures; it's the strong desire to venture into uncharted territories, even if it ruffles some feathers!

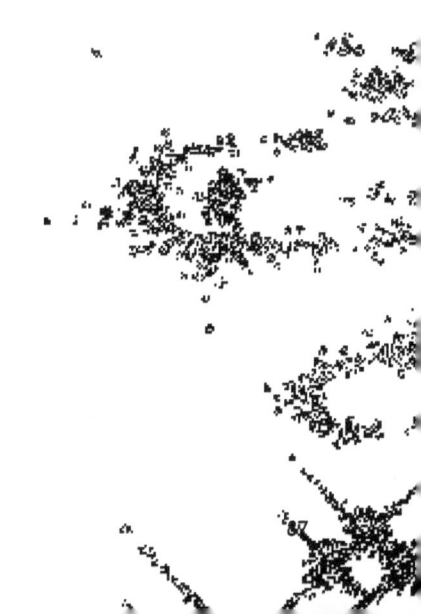

Smallest actions spark the mightiest resolutions!

Start by acknowledging that little thought that tugs at your heart, that discomfort when things seem to fall apart. Embrace the version of yourself that feels true, even if it's different from the norm. It's about painting your life with your unique colors, not just settling for what seems easy. Fight for it with every ounce of your being until your passion keeps flowing, leaving no room for regrets. Your beliefs, your dreams—they are worth every effort, every breath. Believe, revolt against doubts, and roar with the courage of your convictions. Your small actions can spark massive change. Trust in your truth, stand firm, and keep pushing until your voice echoes with the unwavering resolve to shape your world.

And that is what will truly define who you are!

#28

Break Free!

Butterflies with wings tied too tight
Challenging her conscience for knowing what's right

The world has set the pace to kill originality to survive
Not to excel but to make her safe place
amongst her own tribe

The colors of her wings fading through the fight
Wishing to go back in her cocoon and give up her flight

Repeat and Re-belief after me...

I won't let anyone clip my wings.
Like the butterflies struggling with their wings tied too tight, I challenge myself to honor what feels right within. The world might pressure me to conform, urging me to blend in just to find safety among those around me. But I refuse to sacrifice my uniqueness merely to fit in.

The fight to retain my originality may dull my colors, but I won't succumb to the desire to retreat into comfort and give up on my journey. I refuse to let circumstances dim the vibrant hues that make me who I am. I embrace the struggle, knowing that it's a part of my growth. I affirm my right to fly free, to be true to myself, and to seek my own path. My wings may feel tied now, but I won't stop fighting for the freedom to soar. I'll break free from the constraints, unfurl my wings, and paint the sky with the vivid colors of my authenticity.

**Be what feels right within!
Be authentically you!**

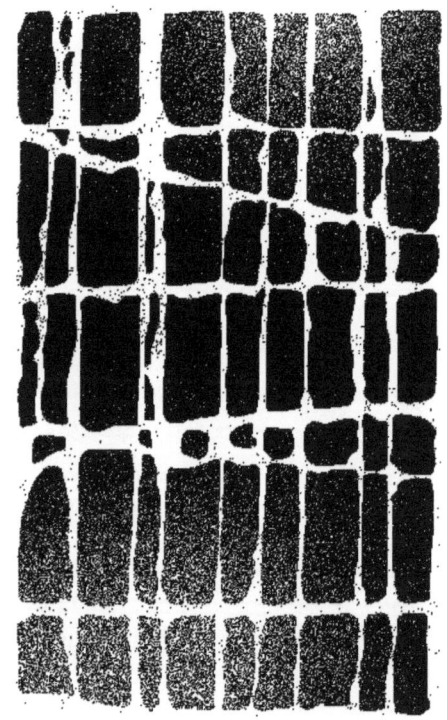

I am the butterfly,
and only I will define how far I fly!

#29

A Special Edition to Strengthen Parent-Child Relationship & Need to Communicate

Because adulthood indeed is defined by childhood experiences!

Horizon - Bridge the Mirage

In the realm where land meets the sea,
a wondrous tale unfolds,
A father and his son, on the shore they stand,
the true nature of beauty, they behold.

Their eyes are drawn to the horizon, where the sky
meets the ocean's hue,
A place where perception weaves its threads,
creating vistas anew.

The horizon, ever-shifting, a mirage of infinite grace,
Defined by where one stands and the angle they embrace.

Yet, as the father raised his weary gaze,
A towering mountain blocked his vision's haze.

He strained his eyes, but could not perceive,
The beauty his son's eyes were quick to believe.

The father, with wisdom etched upon his face,
Sees a mighty mountain standing tall, obstructing nature's chase.

But the child, with innocence untamed,
sees a world so vast and free,
A seagull soaring in the distance, dancing behind the mountain, over the sea.

He points with joy, eyes gleaming, trying to share his view,
Yet the father, towering above, sees nothing but the mountain's imposing cue.

Oh, how the same scene can differ,
through the lens of age and youth,
Perception's glitch, a gentle reminder of life's relentless truth.

The horizon, a metaphor for all walks of life we see,
A reminder to cherish, with empathy,
the perceptions that may be.

In this tale of a father and son,
a lesson gently whispers through,
Bridging the gap of perception is a journey we must pursue.

With understanding hearts and open minds,
we can mend the divide,
By bowing down at times and letting the child's perspective guide.

For in those moments of flexibility,
a world of wonders may appear,
Behind the mountain's lofty veil, a universe so pristine and clear.

Rare seagulls, winged dreams, find their path back home,
seeping in the aquatic aroma,
As the most magnificent sunset paints the sky with
unforgettable vibrant chroma.

The majestic mountain, once perceived as a block,
Transforms into a catalyst, unveiling life's stunning flock.
The horizon remains the same, steadfast and true,
But through the eyes of a child, it glimmers
with a brighter hue.

So let us, as parents, embrace the beauty in
each child's view,
Bowing down with love and perspectives that are new.

For in this dance of perception, we'll find harmony and grace,
And witness the world through their eye,
is a true gift to embrace!

The Horizon of Perception: Bridging the Gap through Communication in Parenting

In the vast expanse of life, our perceptions shape the horizon before us. Just as the angle we stand upon the shore determines what we see, the lens through which we perceive the world is influenced by our situations.

This concept holds true even within the tender bond of a parent and child.

Let us embark on an imaginative journey, where a father and son stand on the shore and discover how the horizon of perception can be bridged through communication, nurturing a beautiful parent-child relationship.

Let's crack deep down into what this poem has to say!

Lesson 1: The Majestic Mountain and the Elusive Sea Gull

The father, with his young son, is marveling at the wonders of nature. The child's eyes sparkle with curiosity as he spots a magnificent seagull soaring behind a distant mountain. Eagerly, he tugs at his father's hand, pointing towards the mesmerizing sight. However, due to the father's height, all he can perceive is the majestic mountain, blocking his view of the gull. This moment paints a vivid metaphor for the gap that often arises between generations. What we perceive as a parent might not always be the best way to vision a situation or react. So, stay open, communicate well, and behold acceptance!

Lesson 2: The Journey of Perception

Just as the father's perspective was limited by his height, in life, age and experiences can create barriers in perceiving the world as our children do. The horizon, seemingly the same for all walks of life, becomes a tapestry of unique interpretations. It is through these perception glitches that misunderstandings and communication gaps take root. However, recognizing the existence of these barriers is the first step toward nurturing a deeper connection. Don't let these communication barriers take charge and create unspoken siloes within the beautiful journey of becoming a confidante to your child. It's the journey of perceptions. So, hold on to each other and bridge the gap together!

Lesson 3: Bowing Down to the Little World

At that moment, the father knelt down and embraced his son's perspective - he saw a brighter and better world. By bowing down, i.e., by showing the flexibility of thoughts, he gained a glimpse into the child's world—a world where seagulls weave paths beyond mountains, painting the sky with their grace. Similarly, in parenting, it is essential for us to bow down, metaphorically, to our children's point of view. By showing flexibility and open-mindedness, we can create an atmosphere of trust and understanding. This will allow you to best analyze and support your child, enhance their capabilities, correct their misconceptions in a more welcoming way, and finally align them to their goals!

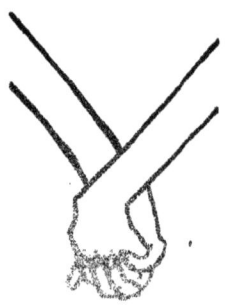

Lesson 4: The Power of Communication

Communication acts as the bridge that spans the gap between generations. As parents, we must strive to communicate with our children effectively, listening and empathizing with their thoughts and feelings. By fostering an environment where they feel heard, valued, and respected, we invite them to share their unique perspective of the world. Through meaningful conversations, we can harmonize our perceptions and celebrate the beauty of diverse viewpoints. So, bridge the gap, be their friends, and hear them out with an open heart!

Lesson 5: Embracing New Worlds

When we embrace our children's perspectives, a whole new world of possibilities opens up before us. Just as the child envisioned rare seagulls dancing against the backdrop of a magnificent sunset, our children hold insights and dreams that can shape our understanding of life. By appreciating their distinct vantage point, we not only bridge the perceptive gap but also enrich our own lives with their vibrant imagination and unfiltered wisdom. So, yes, embrace them wholeheartedly, that's the true art of parenting!

The Essence of Parenting!

Parenting is a journey of constant learning and growth. By acknowledging the horizon of perception, we unlock the power to connect deeply with our children. As we bow down, show flexibility, and communicate fairly, we build a foundation of trust and understanding. Let us embrace the remarkable beauty of the parent-child relationship, where the horizon, though seen differently, unites us in love and appreciation. Through heartfelt communication, we traverse new landscapes together, creating a brighter and more harmonious future for both parent and child.

Remember, when we bow down, we not only see a new world awaiting us behind the mountain but also witness the breathtaking sight of our child's unique vision — a perception that holds the key to unlocking the boundless potential within them and fostering a lifelong connection rooted in love and understanding!

#30

"The True Essence of Living Life is to Strengthen the Bond with Self!"

www.ingramcontent.com/pod-product-compliance
Lightning Source LLC
LaVergne TN
LVHW061619070526
838199LV00078B/7345